Date: 8/22/17

**J 560 JOB
Jobes, Cecily,
Fossils /**

FOSSILS

CECILY JOBES

NEW YORK

Published in 2017 by The Rosen Publishing Group, Inc.
29 East 21st Street, New York, NY 10010

Editor: Caitie McAneney
Book design: Michael Flynn
Interior layout: Reann Nye

Photo Credits: Cover Greg Dale/National Geographic/Getty Images; p.5 Daniel Schoenen/imageBROKER/ Getty Images; p. 7 Taylor Weidman/LightRocket/Getty Images; p. 8 Andrew Lichtenstein/Corbis Historical/ Getty Images; p. 9 Beker/Shutterstock.com; p. 11 Megan R. Hoover/Shutterstock.com; p. 12 Elenarts/ Shutterstock.com; p. 13 Kevin Schafer/Corbis Documentary/Getty Images; p. 14 mj007/Shutterstock.com; p. 15 Olaf Broders Nature Photography/Oxford Scientific/Getty Images; p. 16 Martin Shields/Science Source/ Getty Images; p. 17 Sierralara/Shutterstock.com; p. 19 Stephen J Krasemann/All Canada Photos/Getty Images; p. 21 Barcroft Media/Getty Images; p. 22 Tanaklit Teja/Shutterstock.com.

Library of Congress Cataloging-in-Publication Data

Names: Jobes, Cecily.
Title: Fossils / Cecily Jobes.
Description: New York : PowerKids Press, [2017] | Series: Spotlight on earth
   science | Includes index.
Identifiers: LCCN 2016028152| ISBN 9781499425130 (pbk. book) | ISBN
   9781499425147 (6 pack) | ISBN 9781499425154 (library bound book)
Subjects: LCSH: Fossils--Juvenile literature.
Classification: LCC QE714.5 .J63 2017 | DDC 560--dc23
LC record available at https://lccn.loc.gov/2016028152

Manufactured in China

CPSIA Compliance Information: Batch #BW17PK For further information contact Rosen Publishing, New York, New York at 1-800-237-9932.

CONTENTS

CHAPTER ONE

KEYS TO THE PAST

Fossils are like keys to the past. They tell us what kinds of creatures and plants lived long ago. Fossils are clues that can be studied after a living thing dies and becomes part of the earth.

Some fossils are **preserved** body parts. These are called body fossils. They sometimes look like rocks, but they were once shell or bone. Other fossils are **impressions** in rock. These are called trace fossils. Dinosaur bones are examples of body fossils, while dinosaur footprints are examples of trace fossils. Some fossils, such as the bones of a mastodon, are huge. Others, such as those left behind by bugs and germs, are tiny.

Paleontologists are scientists who study fossils. They discover new fossils all the time. Sometimes they discover new creatures that existed millions of years ago. They use special tools to **investigate** the past.

Trilobites were marine creatures that lived long ago. Trilobite fossils are common, and you can find them near water or in areas that used to be covered by water.

CHAPTER TWO

HOW ARE FOSSILS FORMED?

Not all creatures become fossils after they die. Most remains **decompose** completely. Fossils only form under the right conditions.

Sometimes when a creature dies, its body is buried quickly under **sediment**. Mud and sand are common forms of sediment. This usually happens within a body of water. The soft parts of the creature decompose, including the skin, **organs**, and fur. The hard parts of the animal, such as the bones and teeth, are left behind.

Over time, the bones are pressed between layer upon layer of sediment. Slowly, the hard parts of the animal **dissolve**, leaving a gap in the layers of sediment. Minerals fill the gap and harden into the shape of the bone. This forms a "cast and mold" fossil. People have also found cast and mold fossils of plant parts, such as cones from pine trees.

This cast and mold fossil belongs to an ammonite, which was an ancient marine creature.

Other kinds of fossils are formed through different processes. One of the most common ways fossils are formed is called petrification. In this process, a dead animal is covered in sediment. The soft tissue dissolves and the bones remain. Water soaks the bones, and the minerals in the water fill tiny spaces in the bones. This makes the bones harden into rocklike objects.

Not all fossils are created in marine environments. Some fossils are the remains of animals that have been preserved in ice. Woolly mammoths have been found in ice thousands of years after they died in the Arctic. Other fossils are preserved because the animal died in such a dry place that its remains dried out instead of decomposing. These fossils are often very fragile, or likely to break. They're also very rare and important finds.

WOOLLY MAMMOTH TUSK

Some fossils are preserved in amber, a sticky liquid produced by trees. Amber can harden with bugs inside. Paleontologists have found whole bug bodies that have been preserved in amber for millions of years.

9

SEDIMENTARY ROCK

There are three major kinds of rocks on Earth. Igneous rock is often formed when **magma** reaches Earth's surface, cools, and hardens into rock. Metamorphic rock is formed from the heat and pressure deep inside the earth. Sedimentary rocks are the only rocks that don't form due to heat, and that makes them ideal for preserving fossils.

Sedimentary rocks are made up of tiny bits of sand, stones, and shells. Over time, these bits and pieces form layers and harden into rock. When you look at a sedimentary rock, you may see these individual pieces. Other kinds of sedimentary rock, such as sandstone or shale, may seem smooth. These rocks are made of **particles** of sand or clay. Sedimentary rock is often easy to break or chip apart. If you see a large section of sedimentary rock, you may be able to see the different layers, called strata.

Limestone, mudstone, and flint are all examples of sedimentary rock. This fossil was found in limestone.

CHAPTER FOUR

DINOSAUR FOSSILS

Some of the most famous fossils in the world were formed from the remains of dinosaurs. That's because some of these ancient reptiles were huge and scary. Their fossils help paleontologists learn what these amazing animals may have looked like and how they acted.

If you've ever seen the movie *Jurassic Park*, you may be familiar with the velociraptor. However, this dinosaur looked different than it does in the movie. In 2007, paleontologists used a fossil to prove velociraptors actually had feathers!

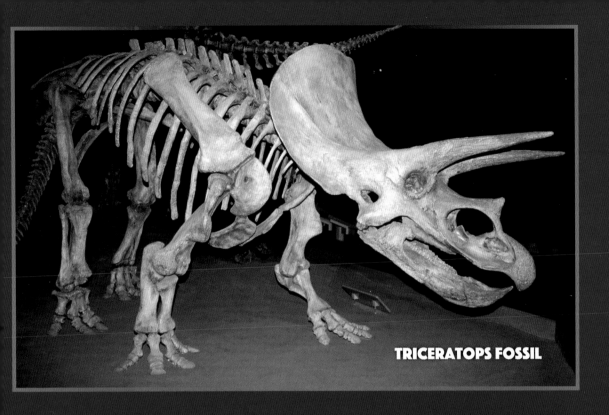

TRICERATOPS FOSSIL

The first nearly complete dinosaur fossil to be found in the United States belonged to a hadrosaur. Paleontologists found this large dinosaur's fossilized skeleton in a mud pit in Haddonfield, New Jersey, in 1858. This was also the first dinosaur to be **reconstructed** for a museum **exhibit**.

In 2014, paleontologists discovered fossils from the largest land dinosaur known to man. This titanosaur was about 122 feet (37.2 m) long. This wasn't a huge predator, though. In fact, its teeth and body structure told paleontologists that it was a herbivore, or an animal that eats only plants.

CHAPTER FIVE

MARINE FOSSILS

Many fossils are found underwater because that's where sedimentary rocks most often form. Most of these underwater fossils were formed from marine animals or plants, although some were formed from animals that were swept into the water. Some marine fossils are found on land in areas that used to be covered by water long ago.

FOSSILIZED MEGALODON TOOTH

This is the fossilized skeleton of a pliosaur, which was a marine dinosaur.

Coral fossils have been found all over the world. Coral polyps are small marine **invertebrates** that sometimes come together to form coral reefs. When paleontologists find coral fossils on land, they know there was once water there.

The largest shark that ever lived—megalodon—left fossils behind that give paleontologists an idea of just how big this fish was. Paleontologists were able to reconstruct a megalodon jaw from fossils. The jaw is around 11 feet (3.4 m) across with more than 180 teeth. Paleontologists think this shark grew to more than 50 feet (15.2 m) long!

CHAPTER SIX

PLANT FOSSILS

Plants can be fossilized, too. Some plant fossils are just impressions of leaves. Fern fossils are quite common. Thicker plant parts, such as roots or stems, may be preserved as cast and mold fossils. In order to reconstruct a full plant, paleontologists often have to find fossils from each part of the plant and then put them together. There are rarely fossils of flowers because their petals are too soft.

Petrified wood is a kind of plant fossil. It forms when trees die and minerals are absorbed, or taken into, the wood. After thousands of years, parts of the wood are replaced with crystals. Petrified wood is often very beautiful because it's made of shiny minerals, such as quartz and amethyst. You can visit the Petrified Forest, a national park in Arizona, to see trees that turned into fossils.

This fossil, which shows an impression of a fern, was found in a coal mine in Pennsylvania.

CHAPTER SEVEN

MASSIVE MAMMAL FOSSILS

Today, the African elephant is the largest land mammal in the world. Fossils tell us that, long ago, other large, elephant-like mammals walked the earth.

Woolly mammoths were massive mammals that roamed northern plains until around 12,000 years ago. They weren't predators and instead preferred to eat grass and other plants. Paleontologists learned that from looking at the shape of their teeth. They had long, curved tusks that grew to about 15 feet (4.6 m) long. They were covered in long, shaggy hair and liked the cold weather of the Ice Age. In 2013, a whole mammoth was found in Siberia, perfectly preserved in the glacial ice.

Mastodons preferred to live in forests and swamps. They were smaller than woolly mammoths but they were also covered in shaggy hair. The mastodon is the official Michigan state fossil because many mastodon fossils have been found there.

This picture shows a woolly mammoth fossil. Notice its long, curved tusks. Woolly mammoths may have used their tusks for digging in the snow and fighting.

CHAPTER EIGHT

HUMANLIKE FOSSILS

Over thousands of years, humans have evolved, or changed, to look the way we do now. Most scientists agree that humans share a common **ancestor** with modern apes. This ancestor existed between 5 million and 8 million years ago. Fossils of early human ancestors tell us what they may have looked like and how they **adapted** over time to their surroundings.

The first humanlike fossil to be found was named Lucy. Lucy was found in 1974 in Ethiopia. Paleontologists could tell this fossil belonged to a female hominid. A hominid is one of the species in the same family that came into being after the human and ape family trees split. They could tell by the skeleton that Lucy could walk upright. She lived around 3 million years ago.

The closest relative to humans was the ancient Neanderthal. The first Neanderthal fossil was found in 1829 in Germany, but it took years to figure out what it was. Neanderthal fossils told paleontologists that these hominids were short and strong.

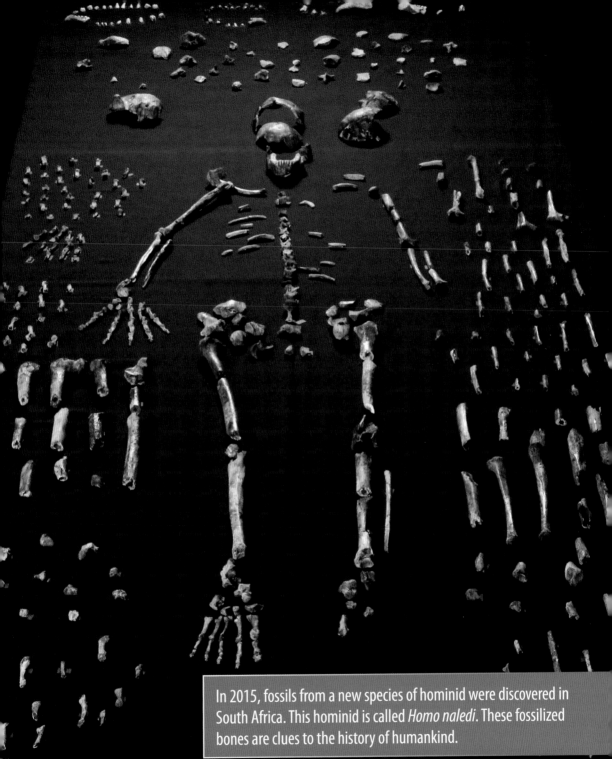

In 2015, fossils from a new species of hominid were discovered in South Africa. This hominid is called *Homo naledi*. These fossilized bones are clues to the history of humankind.

CHAPTER NINE

WHAT DO PALEONTOLOGISTS DO?

Paleontologists have an interesting job because they study both the earth and things that once lived. They need to understand both earth science and life science to piece together the clues that have been left behind. Many paleontologists try to figure out the connections between creatures that once existed and similar ones that exist today. They try to figure out why some species died out. That tells us a lot about the ancient world.

Paleontologists spend time in the field, or outside, and in the lab. They go to areas of the world that are known to have many fossils. They use special tools to dig and sweep dirt away to safely uncover fossils. They identify fossils and bring them back to a lab to test them and possibly find out how old they are. Paleontologists are detectives of the past!

GLOSSARY

adapt (uh-DAHPT) To change in order to better live in a certain environment.

ancestor (AHN-seh-stuhr) An animal that lived before others in its family tree.

decompose (dee-kuhm-POHZ) To cause something to be slowly broken down by natural processes.

dissolve (dih-ZOLV) To mix with a liquid and become part of it.

exhibit (ehk-ZIH-biht) A collection of objects displayed in a public place for people to look at.

impression (ihm-PREH-shun) The stamp, form, or mark that results from contact with a surface.

invertebrate (ihn-VER-teh-brayt) An animal that lacks a spine, or backbone.

investigate (ihn-VEH-stih-gayt) To study deeply.

magma (MAG-muh) Hot, liquid rock inside Earth.

organ (OHR-guhn) A body part that does a certain task.

particle (PAR-tih-kuhl) A very small piece of something.

preserve (preh-ZUHRV) To keep safe.

reconstruct (ree-kuhn-STRUKT) To put something back together.

sediment (SEH-dih-mehnt) Matter, such as stones and sand, that is carried onto land or into the water by wind, water, or land movement.

INDEX

PRIMARY SOURCE LIST

Page 15
Pliosaur skeleton. Reconstructed fossilized skeleton. Fossils found in Australia in 1931. Now kept at Harvard Museum of Natural History, Boston, Massachusetts.

Page 19
Woolly mammoth skeleton. Reconstructed fossilized skeleton. Now kept in Royal Tyrrell Museum of Palaeontology, Alberta, Canada.

Page 21
Homo naledi skeleton. Reconstructed fossilized skeleton. Discovered in 2014 near Johannesburg, South Africa. Now kept at the Evolutionary Studies Institute at the University of the Witwatersrand, Johannesburg, South Africa.

WEBSITES

Due to the changing nature of Internet links, PowerKids Press has developed an online list of websites related to the subject of this book. This site is updated regularly. Please use this link to access the list: www.powerkidslinks.com/soes/fossil